The Circle of Life

The Circle of Life

REVISED EDITION

Andrew Thomas Elder

The Circle of Life.
Copyright © 2019, 2022 by Thomas Andrew Elder.

Originally published by Writers Republic, LLC (2019)

All rights reserved. No part of this book may be reproduced in any form or by any electronic or mechanical means, including information storage and retrieval systems, without permission in writing from the publisher and author, except by reviewers, who may quote brief passages in a review.

This publication contains the opinions and ideas of its author. It is intended to provide helpful and informative material on the subjects addressed in the publication. The authors and publisher specifically disclaim all responsibility for any liability, loss, or risk, personal or otherwise, which is incurred as a consequence, directly or indirectly, of the use and application of any of the contents of this book.

Certain stock imagery © Shutterstock.com.

ISBN: 978-1-63950-145-8   [Paperback Edition]
       978-1-63950-147-2   [Hardback Edition]
       978-1-63950-146-5   [eBook Edition]

Printed and bound in The United States of America.

Gateway Towards Success

1309 Coffeen Avenue
STE 1200, Sheridan,
Wyoming, 82801 USA
 +13179780258
www.writersapex.com

Contents

Preface vii

Acceptance 1
A Good Taste of Life! 3
Already There and Don't Even Know It... 5
Alzheimer's Disease 7
An Example of Art.. 9
Andrew's Epitaph 11
Bearing Crosses Keep on Keep'n' on: Discipline and Tenacity 13
Can Things or Life Get Better? Making Things Better Regardless
   of Who You Are..15
Death and Time..17
Can We Cope without Drugs? Drugs...19
Encouragement 21
Every Thirty Seconds or Less.. 23
Faith 25
Forgiveness... 27
Frank Sr. and Frank Jr. (Francis) 29
Frank Sr. and Frank Jr. (Francis) Continued..................................... 31
Friendship! 34
Gratitude... 36
Gratitude and Humility 38
Hair 40
He Knows What's Going On! 42
Help.. 44
His Name 46
How Much More 48

Ink and Paper	50
Keep On Keep'n' On	52
Keep Trying!	54
Kids	56
Liberty	58
Linguistics	60
Love	63
Manmade Sunshine Can Sunshine Be Man-Made with No Electricity?	65
My Time, My Son, Goin' Fish'n'!	67
Optimism vs. Pessimism	69
Patience and Gratitude	71
Physics and Faith	73
Recycling All Our Stuff, Especially Our Souls	75
Scars	77
Self-Control	79
Self-Forgiveness	81
Shema! The Shema and Its Meaning	83
Stay Well and Safe	85
Tenacity and Persistence	87
The Grid	89
The Piano	91
The Power of Prayer	93
Thought, Words, Action	95
Time and Love	97
Trials and Tribulations	99
Vise/Vice	101
Work	103
Note from the Author	105
About the Author	107

Preface

The Circle of Life is a collection of philosophical poetry, spiritual in nature. It is meant to inspire hope and inspire a glimmer of faith, love, and peace of mind, possibly letting us find these things as we take a look at ourselves and as we ponder and relate to these thoughts. God's speed.

YHWH is God's Name, sounds like YAA WAY and/or YAHUWAH-YHUH. It truly makes it more personal to say His Name. It could be considered sinful not saying His Name in spiritual conversation, not ineffable.

To the unknown author whose quote I used in the beginning of this book right after my first, "Every thirty seconds, or less." This quote, "Remember," in my opinion, truly sets the tone for my thoughts to flow afterward. Thank you.

And to all those who, at the very least, have read "Remember" or heard of it and heeded its words!

DECEMBER 22, 2016

Acceptance

If we don't like something or somebody, do we accept it or them?

When we don't like a given situation or person, we truly only hurt ourselves if we don't accept it or them. We can't change them or whatever, but we can work on ourselves!

Thirty-five years ago, I had become a double amputee. I didn't like it one bit and thought my life was over! What was I going to do now?

After some serious soul-searching, I learned this was just the beginning. I realized that I can't do a lot of things, but I can do a lot of things others can't. This is where I accepted my condition. Never quit trying and accept it, then turn whatever over to HIM.

I still get frustrated, sometimes fall into a rut, but I always manage to pull myself up and carry on with integrity. We can do this if we try!

One of the biggest things that still helps me is when I can humble myself and ask for help. HE knows the kind of help I need and will provide for me if I'm ready.

Amein!

Notes

JULY 27, 2012

A Good Taste of Life!

Life, another beautiful word, our reality being a true gift!

Life is always good, even through trials and tribulations.

It is how we handle these rough spots in life that truly matters.

Life offers growth, or resentment.

Our attitude is contingent on these things.

I never ever would have thought being a double amputee would be a good thing! It is actually a very beautiful blessing! For I have been blessed in overcoming that incident, showing others how my attitude helped me grow.

When one clearly makes a choice of growing rather than living in resentment, the world around us slowly begins to bloom.

Because survival is a basic instinct, one hopefully makes that choice of wanting to live more than having to. This is exactly where spirituality can take root from within!

One more thought to ponder, which greatly helps anything: Acceptance with prayer makes living in life, rather than existing in life, gratefully joyful!

YHWH, bless you and Amein.

Notes

February 2012

Already There and Don't Even Know It

Our faith is a very powerful force. Throughout history, faith has been and still is strong enough to die for. That kind of mind-set is definitely outside the box. The box is our understanding of time and space, here and now. What about outside of that? The more we learn, the less we know. As time carries on, more shall be revealed.

Now what about "there and don't even know it." Where is there? There is the place of the unknown, but known to the one of strong faith! There is the ultimate reality—death. It shall be gloriously fun, but not rush for that to come into being at this time. There's time again, maybe.

What a true blessing to live by the Golden Rule, all the blessings in our everyday life! It's sad to think of Damascus and not living by that rule of doing unto others.

NOTES

October 2016

Alzheimer's Disease

Is there anything we can do when we don't know what's wrong?

How disheartening it is to have a constant watch over one afflicted with Alzheimer's disease. One's brain literally disintegrates, turning from a healthy pink and red color to a dull, lifeless gray, brain-dead. One can function for quite some time but not know anything, even family. That is the worst emotional pain I know! What can one do?

Rightfully, a family member should look after a loved one or have arrangements made for them to be looked after at home.

This is rarely the case due to work or whatever. We need greater respect for the elderly; they raised us. We should return the favor. This is where the faith though works comes into action.

Often all we can do is pray. Never stop praying. A solution shall come.

Amein.

Notes

September 10–20, 2012

An Example of Art

Every one of us has, in some special way, a God-given talent. Your gift can be anything and not even recognized for nearly a lifetime! I turned fifty when I discovered a talent for writing.

I have two sisters, very musically inclined, and a brother with the same profession of nearly forty years.

Painting from sketches, cooking from experience, communication through conversation, writing, classical music, etc., maybe you possess one of these gifts.

When we discover something we're good at and enjoy it, what a blessing it is to share this in His Name.

I recently spoke with a renowned rabbi on my spiritual journey, and we both agreed how blessed we truly are. Although our philosophies may differ, our respect and love for our brothers and sisters standing together under one God is art.

Our talents, whatever they may be, properly utilized, makes one joyous and free.

All our gifts are blessings showing His love for us! Are you utilizing your gift(s)?

YHWH Bless and Amein.

Notes

November 17, 2016

Andrew's Epitaph

Have you ever wondered about the ultimate reality?

Andrew Thomas Elder/Miro'
October 27, 1961–?

Now I am HIS point man. Before when I was here with you, I was only a part-timer, born into sin. Take heed, atone. Amein.

Please don't get me wrong, I don't have any kind of death wish. I should have been killed outright thirty-five years ago. HE had other plans for me, which took about thirty years for me to figure out, and I'm still learning!

I was hit as a pedestrian by a drunk driver, thrown one hundred twenty feet, almost drowned from rib cages puncturing both lungs, took in over one hundred twenty units of blood, and all that was good! My accident happened at the same time hospitals across America were double-checking their blood supply, tainted with the AIDS virus. I spent a half hour in ambulance to the hospital.

Yet here I am writing, a bit more and playing the piano! I gratefully accomplished much since then. Amein.

Notes

September 25, 2016

Bearing Crosses Keep on Keep'n' on: Discipline and Tenacity

Two things come to mind when told of how a child jumped in front of a long rifle being discharged to take the round instead of the intended target: (1) the child was brainwashed to save his comrade(s) no matter what, distraction from line of fire, or (2) the child simply wanted to end everything.

Remember, the child was never the intended target. It was too late while the trigger was being depressed. This was a time of military conflict, never a declared war.

To see and speak with this gentleman, you would never guess he has experienced this, but he has, and then some!

I am grateful for his service to our country, and we joyfully greet each other with "Shalom!" What inner strength! I pray for you, amigo. We all need prayer.

Notes

Thought of December 22, 2014
Written June 20, 2016

Can Things or Life Get Better? Making Things Better Regardless of Who You Are

All of us can make things better. Mom or Dad fix'n' an ouchie.
A friend sharing a cup of coffee with some kind words.

A philanthropist giving needed things for hungry
people. A pastor or rabbi saying comforting words for
thought and action. A helping hand and prayer.

We all can make things better, from you and me
to heads of state, when we work together!

So let us hope and pray we can take our country back as our
heads of state get their act together to make things better for all.

Notes

May 2012

Death and Time

How much time do I have before the ultimate reality?

Only His divine plan will tell.

Am I ready?

I like to think so, but there is so much more to be done.

Will I leave some kind of good contribution for others to ponder?

I hope so, and think I have a fair start as I learn.

Will you be ready?

I pray so!

Notes

Thought of December 2014
Written July 2016

Can We Cope without Drugs? Drugs

What a profound topic! Everywhere you look and everything we
do is somehow drug-related. Addiction. For me, it generally
starts with two cups of coffee and a cigarette, daily. And
four raw almonds with a short snort of aloe vera juice.
It's difficult to describe the gratitude I have in quitting
other vices; I did it with prayer and determination!
I feel much better, but still being selfish and
addicted to the tobacco. Some day.
All I can do is to keep trying!
Never quit trying!
Amein.

Others start
with soda pop, a beer,
a pill, a lost feeling, the need
through addiction to numb a pain, even
if the pain is nonphysical. This is where we should
let and allow Him to help us with our mess. He is always
there for us, but we often don't let anyone in, even Him! So let
us not, through self-inducement, let the sands of our hourglass of life
run out and die prematurely. We have the
gift of choices to help ourselves,
and He will help us if we allow Him in!
Biofeedback helps too, using our mind
over matter! It can work when we try. Hallelujah! Amein.

Notes

February 2013

Encouragement

encourage (tr. v.)

1. To inspire to continue on a chosen course; impart courage or confidence to; embolden; hearten. 2. To give support to; foster.

What is it that encourages us? The number of ways we can be encouraged is simply infinite.

The beautiful times and scenes of a day, sunrise through sunset; the fragrance of dinner cooking after a long day; the good feeling after working out or helping someone out in need. A faint or beaming smile, caring words, or whatever might be encouraging to you!

These and everything encouraging to us are but merely one of YHWH's many ways in showing His Love for us, especially when we do more of His Will as we learn and help each other.

Brotherly love.
Amein.

Notes

November 2011

Every Thirty Seconds or Less

Imagine the face of a clock with a second hand. Watching the second hand fall from the twelve to the six is YHWH's love pouring down upon us, which comes in many forms. And from the six back up to the twelve again is our love to YHWH through prayers, good deeds, helping our brothers and sisters with unconditional love and sharing.

I think He smiles upon me and many, many others like me who try and do better most of the time.

But the time will come, lest the second hand stops, that I be ready! And all my brothers and sisters will be ready too. Thirty seconds, or less.

Remember,

The shortest distance between a problem and a solution is the distance between your knees and the floor. The one who kneels to the Lord can stand up to anything.

—*Author Unknown*

Notes

June 2012

Faith

What is faith? Can I try some?

Wow! What loaded questions! Where do I begin?

Do you recognize opportunity? Often we don't recognize opportunity or are too late in doing so. Do you have faith in me? Please think of me merely a messenger.

Faith, not being tangible, must come from within. How a seed is planted, only He knows. It is truly beautiful as it takes root and grows, especially if you are blessed to witness such an event. More so, as we feel that growth!

"Faith must be cultivated," as my father shared with me when I was ready, being ready in thought, prayer, and deed. Dad finished, saying, "Pray for faith." I also remember being told,

"Be careful what you pray for, you might just get it!"

Amein!

Notes

October 2012

Forgiveness

To forgive one who has wronged us is not an easy task, but it can be done! Reflecting upon myself, I remember very well making a mountain out of a molehill.

Back then, this mountain was justifiable; I had to become a double amputee from being hit by a drunk driver. Forgiveness was not even a thought!

I soon gratefully became aware just how blessed I really am to have lived through such a catastrophic event! As time passed on, I slowly began to grow in newly discovered faith.

Reflecting on my life before my accident, gave me a second chance even when He knew of all my sins and transgressions and blessed me to live again! Only then was I able to ask for His forgiveness and then forgive myself without ever forgetting!

Forgiving myself first made it easier to forgive anyone else. Those who do not forgive suffer more than the one who offended.

Now in the present, knowing how some people have been raised and knowing nothing else, I am able to forgive and not forget so as not to repeat history. Slowly, I became teachable. Amein.

"So repent of this wickedness of yours, and pray to the Lord. Perhaps you will yet be forgiven for holding such a thought in your heart. For I see that you are extremely bitter and completely under the control of sin!" (Acts 8:22–23)

Notes

November 28, 2016

Frank Sr. and Frank Jr. (Francis)

Do we know and are we truly grateful for what our nation's veterans have done and do for us?

These are two gentlemen I had the privilege serving under in a state reserve unit. They are both battle-hardened veterans who served our country in the early '60s in Southeast Asia. They are also twin brothers, and it is noteworthy reiterating their experiences.

Francis served with the USMC, Force Recon, and was the only man out of a six-man recon group to come back alive. They paired up, and two went here, two went there, and Francis and his partner were deep in the jungle when Francis's partner whispers to him, "I have to go [void]." Francis whispers back, "Okay, hurry up." He knew something was wrong after five minutes when his partner didn't show up. He lay there in that spot for seventy-two hours! And crawled out with the birds. He remembered hunting with his father and being told, "When the birds are chirping, move slow. When the birds stop, you stop. Lay low!"

Francis remembers this at age eighteen, fresh out of boot camp, halfway around the world, deep in jungle and alone! He made it back to base camp three months later and debriefed. This is taught to this day. Thank you, Top. That is how he is addressed—Top Sergeant! Unless he told you, "Top is okay."

Notes

November 28, 2016

Frank Sr. and Frank Jr. (Francis) Continued

Frank Sr., I feel, is my best friend outside of my father. He is a retired lieutenant colonel from our state reserve unit. He served with the Big Red One, 101st Airborne Division, US Army, before he came back home and served again in the reserves. His MOS, or military operation of service, was to disrupt the flow of logistics along the Ho Chi Minh Trail.

This one particular mission, everything was set, wired tight with booby traps, remote-control claymores—the works. It was a successful mission. Few survivors at the end of the supply line.

Frank and his partner's position compromised when helicopter extract took place. They were about four hundred yards away from the site, but the few survivors were taking random potshots at them since the enemy could not get a good bead on Frank and the helicopter as he climbed Jacob's ladder. He said he would hear an occasional round whiz by.

He then tried to hold this ladder steady for his partner, which was difficult due to the rotor wash. His partner frantically tried to grab it as he jumped to do so several times. Frank then saw him climb on something and was able to grab Jacob's ladder as they were successfully extracted!

Frank told him he saw him climb up on something but couldn't see and asked him about it. He said he didn't know, it wasn't there and then was there, invisible but solid enough to climb on and securely grab the rope ladder! At this point, as Frank is telling me this experience, he starts getting choked up, and I felt goose bumps on my right stump! Frank told me his name, but I cannot remember, but I won't forget Frank!

I gratefully served with them in our state reserve unit eleven years after my accident, three and a half tours or ten and a half years. I like to say, "My war with a drunk driver. I lost the battle, but I'm winning the war!" Divine intervention, both counts.

YHWH with Frank and his partner and with me being carried one hundred twenty feet.

HE's with all of us if we quiet ourselves and seek!

Notes

May 2012

Friendship!

What a treasure to have true friendship!

The way to have such a treasure starts with the three basics, as with any relationship: communication, honesty, and trust, in this order.

Keep it simple and exactly like this, and you too will find treasure!

One is blessed to have but a handful of true friends!

We should know this, or will shortly.

YHWH bless!

Notes

December 6, 2016

Gratitude

Are we truly grateful for what little we have?

It truly is difficult to describe my gratitude for what little I have. I hope and pray that you do too! There was a time when I was rather bitter and thought of suicide. Gratefully that thought was short-lived instead! At that particular point in time, I had somewhat of a conscience and couldn't bear the thought of my mother finding me, like, dead!

This is when I was so desperate that I asked HIM for help. Being exhausted, I slept well that night and started the next day with a question: What can I do to make things better?

It has been a very long row to hoe, but that's what it took to get me where I am today. Believe me, it hasn't been easy because I have a talent for doing things the hard way.

Humility and being able to ask for help from my brothers and starting a wonderful spiritual journey made all the difference!

So when I lost everything, I was actually given an opportunity to start over, literally start over from scratch—learning how to walk again, tying my shoes with one hand, and living in a new residence, etc.

Today, I occasionally get frustrated but cannot or will not allow man to get under my skin. Gratefully my biggest frustration is taking forever learning piano sheet music written for one hand. It's as tough or as easy as we make it. Amein!

Notes

August 2012

Gratitude and Humility

God is great, God is good,

And I thank Him for my "hood."

This is, of course, my neighborhood.

I truly thank YHWH today; I can love my neighbors as I would myself. Sometimes this is really impossible. Now is the time when I, at the very least, remember to pray for them. Anger is a total waste of time and energy. Goodness can be done in this way if I try!

Amein!

Notes

JANUARY 2013

Hair

Most pictures of Christ (Yahushua) show Him with long hair.
Even though I too wear my hair long, I am Christ-like (Messiah-like)
most of the time. I'm a sinner. I have atoned past sins
and do not repeat them, but new ones pop up.

It truly is never-ending, temptations that arise.
Today I also have the gift of choices to be made,
gratefully they too are healthier, just for today.
I'll deal with tomorrow when and if it comes.

It is my thought processes that matter most
and the actions I take, including the words
coming out of my mouth.

I leave you with a thoughtful prayer,
to have a great hair day.
Especially and always
with Him!

Amein.

Notes

April 2012

He Knows What's Going On!

Is he Big Brother? Or

Is He YHWH?

The answer is both my friend, take heed!

My father often told me,

"Hope for the best, prepare for the worst,
and take whatever comes."

Dad was gratefully instrumental in my growing faith.

Thanks, Dad!

Mom always reminded me to "Keep an
open mind." Thank you, Mom!

Between both my parents, I have gratefully developed a
God-given talent in sharing my thought(s) with you.

Thank you!

Notes

July 3–4, 2012

Help

What kind of help do we need?

As a country, it is almost out of reach. As
individuals, we need all the help we can get!

I believe knowing our limitations makes us stronger
to humble ourselves in asking for help.

When listening to friends complain and talk of their troubles,
we should intervene and tell them to "please stop." It is
too draining of time and energy. It brings one down!

We shall focus on solutions with good intent and prayer.
For if we don't, it will only cause discontent through tear!

When we came together as done in World War II, it was
done and can be again through cause, faith, and
unity. Time shall tell as to what is to be.

Buckle up!

Notes

July 2012

His Name

Blessed is His Name! How is He referred to? Do you understand who I am referring to? YHWH.

Are we grateful for His love for us? Lord only knows how many times I wasn't! I thank YHWH for His forgiveness, and love for me too!

How or what is our intent when we say His Name? I sadly remember when my intentions were rather sad too.

I truly feel relief when talking and speaking His Name with Him today.

Thank You, YHWH.

I still pray that more of us feel this way too!

Gratefully and thankfully, follow His Name today with Amein.

Notes

September 29, 2012

How Much More

How much more can we take? A group, a community, a family, or an individual?

How much more devastation can we seemingly take? Most of our devastation seems to be such, seemingly devastating; however, true devastation makes my being a double amputee look like merely a flesh wound!

When we take time and really look from within, we can't help but see most of our needs being met. Again, looking deep from within, we sometimes need to remember gratitude for everything else, all the little or not-so-little stuff we have all around us.

Some stuff, little and big, might be such things as a full belly, a roof overhead, transportation, just to mention a few!

In this place of looking within, we may find a twinkle of light. A glimmer we may call hope or faith that things will be better. Time itself can and does heal as well. As you begin to grow, things around you will grow with "pray and believe."

Time, as I once allowed, staying consistent in prayer and belief, my glimmer of light slowly and gratefully turned into faith, which is priceless today!

Things do get better, when I try to do more! No matter what happens, we can take it! Especially in those close calls when our life flashes before our eyes, we should have faith and believe all will be well. May the love of our LORD be with you now and always!

Notes

August 2012

Ink and Paper

As a writer of poetry, a very dear and
special friend shared with me,

"Before a word is written, you are master of it.
Once a word is written it is master of you."

I could not agree more. It has also made me think of
a proper name and word too, and then some:
YHWH

What a beautifully divine Hebrew Name/Word,
a Word to not just consider but live with.

Amein.

Notes

December 8, 2016

Keep On Keep'n' On

Do we often worry too much about the future?

Sometimes, if not often, we worry too much! To do such is a total waste of time and energy.

It's all too common to have concerns about a disgruntled loved one or family member. When we have talked and pleaded to no end, sought a third party, perhaps even professional help, we then need to turn it over to HIM and pray for this individual(s).

We must take care of ourselves first before we can offer help to anyone. We can't give what we don't have.

To worry or be fearful is exactly what the enemy wants, and it is often difficult to love thy enemy.

This is why today, just for today, I employ a new philosophy: Keep on keep'n' on!

And always try to do the right thing! The future will take care of itself.

Amein.

Notes

August 2012

Keep Trying!

How? How does one carry on after something catastrophic?

From where I once stood and actually lay
before, there was no direction but up.

It took absolutely all my energy from time to time, I
wanted to live more than I did to give in! And die.

I remember well talking with and asking Him for help. He
heard my plea—Amein!—and blessed me with my need(s).

Truly He helps when one but asks Him with humility.

There surely is not enough room here for
me to lay out all His blessings.

Starting with living through my ordeal, being
blessed with life again, which is the best!
Medically speaking, it truly is miraculous!

Life is really spectacular, especially as I feel that
humility when able to help someone else in need.

Amein.

NOTES

December 25, 2016

Kids

Do you have children?
I have three kids: Mathew, who is waiting on me;
Misty; and Sunny. Mathew is my son, who never drew
a breath of our air—premature child birthing. It was
tough at first, and I think of him often, wondering.

My other two kids have four legs and tails, my
dogs. They are just like kids; they talk back,
use selective hearing, and are spoiled.

At this point in time, it's difficult to know who raised
who! I am very grateful to them because I don't know
how many times they have kept me on my paws!

I've had numerous pets over the years, but these two are just like
and are my kids! Misty made the back cover with me on my first
book, and again with Sunny on my second. What a blessing!

Thank you, Misty and Sunny!

See ya soon, Mathew.

Amein.

Notes

Liberty

Liberty, what a beautiful word.

A word and way of life to die for.

A reward and time for personal temporary leave of duty,
whether from service to our country, job, or life itself.

It is truly sacred.

Especially when spent with a loved one! One
might call that heaven on earth.

Enjoy and carry on!

Notes

August 10, 2016

Linguistics

Have you ever thought of a word's origin?

At one point in time early on, all peoples spoke one language, Hebrew, then it was splintered into all the languages spoken today, but proper names and nouns were not translated.

I have always been interested in history, and about a decade ago, I became more interested in the history of our faith. Through research, development, and relative consistence in my homework, I have discovered proper names before they were translated. Again, if you remember learning English, proper names and nouns are not to be translated.

These names are most important, being (1) His Name, (2) His Son, (3) His Spirit, and (4) prayer confirmation. In Hebrew, they are as follows:

1. YAHUWAH—YHUH (or) YHWH
2. Yahushua—Yashua
3. Ruach Hakodesh
4. Amein

The following are also acceptable after translation, and grammatically so:

1. GOD
2. Jesus
3. Holy Spirit
4. Amen

Hi, my name is Andrew/Andy. I'm a member of Messianic Anonymous, and I don't know everything. There's probably a larger list, but these four are very important. We're all in this boat together. This is a lifetime learning process. Thank you, YHUH/YHWH!

Notes

December 18, 2016

Love

Do we freak out when someone says "I love you!" or do we know what love is?

Do we actually know what love is? I had a difficult time with this, as so many of us do. Why? Because we were raised in a dysfunctional environment. We grew up not knowing what love is and had the wrong idea about love altogether.

Love starts in our heart, then proceeds to our mind. When we have been hurt enough, and hopefully overcome that obstacle to learn from the mistakes we made, to accept, whether our fault or not, is when we can be ready—ready to learn about love, that love is much more than a romantic feeling.
It includes brotherly love, which is often misinterpreted when saying it, the meaning, unconditional, and brotherly love.

We cannot love anybody if there is hate in our heart, so we then need to deprogram ourselves to get the hate out of our heart that we may learn about love, HIS love for us!

Then loving ourselves first, we have a chance at finding true love!

Notes

October 2016

Manmade Sunshine Can Sunshine Be Man-Made with No Electricity?

As you might know, it takes more facial
muscles when we frown or grimace.

And when we do just the opposite and see family,
a friend, or better yet a complete stranger do
this, then man-made sunshine is evident.

SMILE!

Amein!

Notes

March 2013

My Time, My Son, Goin' Fish'n'!

In my time here in this reality, I have not yet had the privilege of meeting my son. Since he never drew a breath of our air, I shall expire my last breath before meeting him.

And we shall meet on His Golden shore, with the rest of my family and friends!

I hope and pray we all get as much of His will done here and now. We gotta try before we get home. Regardless, He will greet us with open arms for us to learn more.

Once we're all settled in our new home, we can head for a couple of good fish'n' holes along Lick Creek, where I grew up. It'll be great fun!

Hope you know of a good fish'n' hole or two. If you don't, I can show you one around the bend so we don't get our lines tangled when we meet again!

Praise be to YHWH. Shabbat Shalom!

Notes

JUNE 2012

Optimism vs. Pessimism

Optimism:
1. A tendency or disposition to expect the best possible outcome or to dwell upon the most hopeful aspects of a situation.
2. Philosophy.
    a. The doctrine asserted by Leibnitz that our world is the best of all possible worlds.
    b. The belief that the universe is improving and that good will ultimately triumph over evil.

Pessimism:
1. A tendency to take the gloomiest possible view of a situation.
2. The doctrine or belief that this is the worst of all possible worlds and that all things ultimately tend toward evil.
3. The doctrine or belief that the evil in the world outweighs the good.

Another profound concept—to have experienced both and carry on with the optimist view, to live life to its fullest despite failing, learning from mistakes, carrying on. That in itself is worthy of feeling good about, with better choices made in the process. A little prayer can go a long way that can turn into faith—faith in Him and faith in ourselves! All we need do is but ask. It may or may not be immediate, but a solution shall come.

I would have and thought of giving up long ago if it were not for a glimmer of faith. As it grows, so does my need for more of His will through works! Faith without works is dead. I was dead for too long. Life is what we make of it. It is always good as we honestly try.

Carry on. Shalom.

Amein.

Notes

May 2012

Patience and Gratitude

Patience and gratitude touch every part of life, which must also be cultivated. I remember when I had neither. Clutched in depression, I didn't really want to die and remembered to ask Him for help with a prayer. And He knows the kind of help we need.

As I started to cultivate patience with good intention and prayer, I slowly became more grateful for what little I had and more aware. He heard my prayer(s)! All we need do is but ask.

I often have to remind myself of those earlier days, when faced with adversity and challenge every other day! Truly I am blessed when remembering prayer, patience, and gratitude.

Asking Him for help makes me stronger and more grateful! Patience and gratitude really go hand in hand, which took patience to finally accept and understand.

Can you see how patience and gratitude
really touch every part of life?

Notes

Sept ember 1, 2016

Physics and Faith

Have you wondered about how everything works?

Some twenty-five years ago, for the National Endowment of Arts and Science, on public broadcasting television, a famous scientist said, "Everything that we know of physics is so mathematically perfect, that Divine thought and intervention must be behind it!"

For a scientist to make such a statement some hundred years ago would have been perhaps the end of his career. Today, we can see how and why these things are coming together.

Discoveries are being made and realized in outer space, far beyond our own galaxy!

Archaeological finds are being made as mentioned in the Bible!

Miracles done, most witnessed!

Need I go on?

Faith.

Notes

October 2016

Recycling All Our Stuff, Especially Our Souls

Do you recycle your plastic, aluminum, etc.? All your stuff?

We go through and make enough trash to stretch around the moon and back again, and by this time probably twice, or to Mars and back. Even though I recycle everything, it probably doesn't amount to much, but every little bit counts. I feel like I've made a contribution, no matter how small, and for me, that's a good feeling!

Now how does one go about recycling one's soul? For me, it began with the interest of history into the history of our faith! I'm sure you've heard "Seek and ye shall find." If we are looking for truths, and answers, then you will hopefully find what I have.

This can be as easy or as hard as we make it on one's journey in finding answers and real truths. I find them in His Good Book and in the Torah! "What's that?" you may ask.

"Seek and ye shall find," and feel good about it. I do!

Notes

OCTOBER 2, 2016

Scars

Can we cope with or accept our scars?

These are often difficult to accept but can be and should be! However, they run deep, especially the scars that are not visible. Time can and does heal all wounds, but sometimes not easily. How they are acquired is what makes them profound.

Scars never go away, always there, but can we live with them? Hopefully we can and should, but never forget. This is where acceptance plays its role.

I was not happy becoming a double amputee due to being hit by a drunk driver as a pedestrian and should have been killed outright, but I slowly discovered HE had other plans for me.

That's a perfect example of a domestic scar, along with others that you don't see—abuse, divorce, the loss of a child. Inner strength!

Scars of war go deeper than all mentioned above!
They too can be overcome with inner strength.
We can overcome anything with HIS help.

Amein.

Notes

June 30, 2012

Self-Control

n. Control of one's emotion, desires, or actions by one's own will. Self-controlled (adj.)

Self-control is knowing right from wrong. A simple statement complicated through justification of gray area. Oh, how I have done such, but I am finally listening better to my conscience.

My will has landed me in trouble more than once, until I started trying His Will. I still make mistakes, but not as often, and today I learn from my experiences. I became teachable!

Getting into and seeking more truths through His Word helps greatly when I get into it. The allowance of distractions hinders my growth. One small piece of scripture that has and still helps me is 1 Peter 4:1–11.

I believe this to be the root of all control issues and sound guidance. Self-control through faith offers life! I have written about my greatest weakness, or strength, and deal with her as best I can!

Never quit trying in doing the right thing!

Amein.

Notes

October 2016

Self-Forgiveness

Have we forgiven others who wronged us?

Just as important, have we forgiven ourselves?

When you stop and think about it, you will hopefully realize that if we do not forgive someone who has wronged us, we are the ones who suffer more than the one who offended. Is it because our feelings were hurt? Yes, many times, but who cares? No one!

This is no reason to relive an awkward moment that can turn into an unhealthy resentment or guilt! This can be the onset of health issues such as ulcers, high blood pressure, depression, etc.

All this can be avoided through forgiveness of self. How? When one is spiritually enlightened and asks for HIS Forgiveness, atonement. It may be our lifestyle that leads to the problem. Pray for our enemies!

This is exactly how I kept from harboring resentment. To be totally honest, at first my prayers were distempered toward an individual who wronged me. I soon felt guilt and remorse for praying such thoughts and started praying good change for this individual who wronged me! After praying for positive change a few more days, I soon forgot about the whole thing!

Amein.

Notes

November 21, 2016

Shema! The Shema and Its Meaning

"Hear, O Yisra'el: YHWH our Elohim, YHWH is one! [pause]

"And you shall love YHWH your Elohim with all your heart, and with all your being, and with all your might. [pause]

"And these Words which I am commanding you today shall be in your heart, [pause] and you shall impress them upon your children, and shall speak of them when you sit in your house, and when you walk by the way, and when you lie down, and when you rise up, [pause] and shall bind them as a sign on your hand, and they shall be as frontlets between your eyes. (pause) And you shall write them on the doorposts of your house and on your gates. (pause) And you shall love your neighbors as yourself" (Deuteronomy 6:4–9 and Leviticus 19:18).

Have we forgot about this or just put it on the shelf?

You really don't hear this prayer much any more these days—sad.

The pause is to think about these Words, HIS Words.

Think about it, and maybe it'll grow
on ya, as it is for me. Amein!

Notes

December 15, 2016

Stay Well and Safe

We All Want to Stay Well and Be Safe
Stay well and be safe always, and especially with HIM.

Here and now,

Then and when, YHWH always.

Amein.

Notes

September 15, 2016

Tenacity and Persistence

Have you ever wondered about how one carries on?

I am not a bad example of this. An acquaintance who practically makes me look like it's nothing when in all actuality it really is!

What she has done and does is commendable! She raised her children, who are now in college, making sure they never miss out on Thanksgiving dinners and other holidays. She works two jobs, approximately sixty hours a week, raises Great Danes, and cares for her mother, all the while fixing a country house and doing garden and lawn work. Wow!

My scars are clearly visible as a double amputee, and there are some that you don't see, as we all have. I have overcome and accomplished much.

We all have scars that are hidden, not visible, which is deeper than most want to know but should know. This is part of how one adapts, overcomes, and inspires those we meet who ask us.

Everything we all do, whether it's starting a business, trying to deal with a tough job, divorce, anything in life we may find challenging, builds/develops tenacity and persistence!

We truly can carry on with these!

Amein.

Notes

THOUGHT OF DECEMBER 2014
WRITTEN JULY 2016

The Grid

Have you ever wondered about being off the grid?

Having done plat drawings of properties and one day seeing old cement posts on a country road as property corner markers got my mind thinking: *Original county property markers for a map being the start of the grid even before telephone poles! What advances man has made making the grid what it is today, wow!*

Some folks live off the electrical grid and use alternative power sources, like wind or solar, but are still on the grid through physical addresses and phones. And that's great because who doesn't like to save monies for special occasions? I try to be a penny-pincher!

Then there are some who are completely off the grid, by choice or right, and must be dependent on resources and all logistics for survival. That could be a hard life, as our forefathers may have experienced.

Makes me grateful for what little I have and where I'm at in life!

Then there is One Who cares greatly and knows every inch of HIS grid and our every thought.

Amein.

Notes

November 20, 2016

The Piano

Can or do you play a musical instrument?

To play a musical instrument of any kind helps strengthen our brain, which in turn decreases the risk of Alzheimer's disease.

I learned this fact after one or two years of taking piano lessons at age fifty-one. I did as a kid, but became more interested in life than practicing the piano. Now I thought it would be a fun challenge, especially since I would be playing pieces written for one hand.

It's not just inspiring for me but to those who hear me making a joyful sound with one hand when it sounds as if I'm using two.

I started out with one gig at a community meal, graduated to four gigs at retirement homes and one senior center. As an elder, I'm in like Flynn!

You really can do anything you set your mind to. And it's a lot easier with HIS help! All you have to do is but humbly ask.

Fun gratifying works, at least that's how I did it.

Amein!

Notes

August 2012

The Power of Prayer

Prayer, what a powerful force, especially when one feels
His grace through others praying for someone in need!

One of His many miraculous ways of loving us!

When two or more are gathered in His Name, His
Spirit, Ruach Hakodesh, is always present.

He hears our private prayers too. Do be mindful of
what you pray for. Expect the unexpected.

Prayers are answered when one is ready.
Humility is one way of readiness.

Never stop praying, for He has and is blessing us
every day! One day He may be calling us to do more
of His will or to just come home to Him.

We need to ready ourselves and be in better tune with Him!

Amein.

Notes

THOUGHT OF DECEMBER 2014
WRITTEN JULY 2016

Thought, Words, Action

Often we don't think before we speak, I know I haven't always.

Our thoughts are often followed by words and then action. If we think of a cup of coffee, we usually take action in getting a cup and speak of it in the presence of company. That is like clockwork for me.

When emotionally charged, good or bad, it's imperative to think before we speak. This helps greatly in keeping us out of glue, or trouble. We know this!

It is generally after the fact that we analyze and wish we had not said this or done that. Now is the time for a piece of humble pie! In most cases, it's never too late for an apology, uplifting words.

In some cases, all we can and should do is
pray never to let that happen again.

Amein.

Notes

JUNE 2012

Time and Love

Oh, how we are blessed when these things come together.

When this happens, does it not say it all?

What true blessings we have, and yet with more to come!

What a concept, what faith!

Notes

APRIL 2012

Trials and Tribulations

Inspired by and dedicated to Junior

All of us, that's everyone still breathing, and those before us,
have at the very least dealt with some kind of trauma in life.

How does one go about dealing
with such trials and tribulations?

It truly is not blowing in the wind.
The answer is much, much more than that.
Relationship with YHWH, it is!

I know this from personal experience,
as does anyone who has tried research and development.

Speaking of relationship, 1 Peter 4:1–11

I write and speak this because of my semihumble attitude:
semi due to my faults, yet selfish in my growing faith!

Notes

November 13, 2016

Vise/Vice

Do we use a vise on a workbench or a vice in other ways?

Every day except Saturday, I use a vise on a workbench with a nail in it to punch a hole in the bottom husks of two ears of corn. I then put these on a board with two nails in it, for squirrels.

The one vice I have is much better than other vices I used to have! It's hard to describe the relief I feel from giving these other vices to HIM!

Vice, by definition, is not a good thing.

I've often heard, "Everyone has a vice."

As a double amputee, my body has been through enough abuse, both self-inflicted with vices and not. Perhaps put that in your pipe and smoke it—not!

You don't have go through what I did, but that's what it took to get me where I am today. In other words, don't go about whatever the hard way. All we have to do is ask HIM to help us and want it!

Amein.

Notes

July 14, 2012

Work

As one knows, one must work to survive. Whether it be work at a job, survival, under orders, work must be done. Doing such in today's world takes just as much intestinal fortitude as Special Forces personnel.

One could easily be considered as special when supporting family! As half the country is unemployed, it is important to remember and stay constructively busy, especially when enduring such hardship.

Volunteer work for good causes helps too, one small part in staying constructively busy.

It's imperative to remember YHWH telling Abraham, "I am your shield." It is just as important to remember we all are children of Abraham!

Fear is not an option, only the enemy.

Fortitude is evident when supporting family with little more than faith itself because that kind of faith is works offering life, being His Hands and Feet. It is all in His Hands. Through Him is life, which we barely understand.

One does understand more with strong faith, through His works!

Amein.

Notes

Note from the Author

Dear Mrs. Grill,

I can't thank you enough for enabling me to make a more joyful sound to our Lord and inspire not only myself, but those hearing me play the piano. And it's much more inspiring when people see I made those joyful sounds with one hand when it sounds like I'm using two! Thank you!

Sincerely,
Andrew T. Elder

Mrs. Grill writes music for handy-capable people like myself. In the spring of this year, my music teacher, Hyla Sharrock, met her and got one of her music books autographed for me!

"Enjoy! Joyce Grill."

About the Author

Andrew is a regular guy who had to relearn life as a double amputee at nineteen years of age! He hopes to inspire you with topics that he has, and he is learning about life and a bit more.

www.ingramcontent.com/pod-product-compliance
Lightning Source LLC
Chambersburg PA
CBHW060404080526
44583CB00012B/459